The Refugee C[illegible]
Through the Eyes of the Children

Lesbos, Greece April - November 2015

Robin and Robert Jones

Introduction by
Debra Linesch, PhD, MFT, ATR-BC
Chair, Graduate Department of Marital and
Family Therapy, Loyola Marymount University

ISBN 978-1-883423-47-6

First Edition
10 9 8 7 6 5 4 3 2 1

Edited by Cathy Feldman
Cover & Book Design by Cathy Feldman & Robin Jones
Book Production by Blue Point Books

Written by Robert Jones
Photographs by Robin Jones

The production of this book was sponsored by the Avi Schaefer Fund in memory of Avi Schaefer
www.avischaeferfund.org

Proceeds from the sales of this book will be donated to:
IsraAID: www.israaid.co.il

Published by Blue Point Books
P.O. Box 91347
Santa Barbara, CA 93190-1347
800-858-1058
bpbooks@west.net • www.bluepointbooks.com

Printed in the United States of America

Foreword

In the summer of 2015 our lives and the lives of hundreds of thousands of our fellow human beings were changed. The world was experiencing one of the most inhumane wars of modern times in Syria and generations of people were being forced to flee their homes and their country.

In the seeming hopelessness of their frightening situation a voice of hope rang out. That voice was a promise and a guarantee of safety. That voice, intended or not, started a movement of people for which no one was prepared. That voice was a call from the European Union, primarily the countries of Northern Europe, that answered prayers and awakened dreams. It was an invitation to begin a better life for yourself and more importantly, for your children. All you had to do was get there.

Lesbos, our second home for over forty years, was at the epicenter of a new type of human migration. What was initially a call to help the refugees from war-torn Syria became a call answered by multitudes looking for a better life. The call was answered from as far away as Pakistan, war-weary Afghanistan, Somalia, Iraq and Eritrea. As land routes began to disappear from the Middle East and North Africa, water crossings became the only possibility of reaching the northern EU. The islands of Lesbos, Kos, Samos and Chios were within eyesight of the Turkish mainland where most of the migrants were gathering. The route by sea quickly became the only way to escape the hell of war and poverty.

As the overcrowded rubber rafts began to arrive on our island we were awed at the joy on many faces, a joy that overshadowed the suffering that had launched the refugees on the dangerous water crossings from Turkey. Their faces, exhausted from the journey, beamed with possibility and a feeling of absolute relief that their decision to try for a new future was the right one.

Among the many faces of the thousands who were landing on the islands of Greece, the brightest smiles of all were those of the countless children who came hand-in-hand with parents, grandparents, brothers and sisters. These were children walking in wet clothing, children carried on the backs of brave fathers, children clasping to their mother's long dresses as they trudged uphill in the summer sun. It was in the eyes of these children that we, Robin and I, took refuge from the tsunami of events that were unfolding around us. While we might otherwise feel helpless, the children gave us the courage that we could do something to help in small ways to alleviate the suffering buffeting our island.

Art was Robin's way of offering a moment of relief to the many children arriving on the beach or entering the temporary chaos of the transit camps. Art was here; art was now. The photos and drawings on the following pages are fully in the moment. Robin saw a way for the children to step outside the harsh reality of their current situation. All of the drawings and photos were done within hours of arrival. The simple act of drawing concentrated the children's thoughts on a quieter world where they could express what they were experiencing or, for a moment, to just have a little fun.

Our goal since our return from Greece is to place a human face on this world event and meaning to the term "refugee." This ongoing crisis is changing the world. It is our belief there is an urgent need to educate and offer an opportunity for people to connect to the human side of this tragedy. Fear is confusing and closing many people's hearts. Our motivation is to shed new light through *The Refugee Crisis: Through the Eyes of the Children.*

It was with multiple acts of kindness on a daily basis that the spirit of helping fellow human beings set an example to inspire thousands to care. People around the world heard the call, sent support and helped raise awareness about what was happening.

We want to especially acknowledge and thank the residents of Molyvos and the island of Lesbos, along with the countless local and individual foreign volunteers and aid groups who helped on the front lines 24/7. Without all of you everything would have been completely different for the 400,000+ human beings who arrived on our shores.

Robert and Robin Jones
Santa Barbara, CA/Molyvos, Lesbos
August 2016
www.throughtheeyesofthechildren.com

Introduction

Debra Linesch, PhD, MFT, ATR-BC

The Refugee Crisis: Through the Eyes of the Children became a project that engaged my heart and mind as soon as I met Robin and Robert Jones. The magnitude of the story that they had stepped into was both daunting and inspiring. As they had not turned away from its call, neither could I. I am grateful to Robin who recognized the art process as a way to support and document the children's experiences and to Robert whose compelling narrative contextualizes the tragedy that unfolded.

My own observations are grounded in a commitment to imagery as meaning making and voice enhancing. I have seen the power of art made by children who have been neglected, abused, traumatized and silenced. I know that art can soothe, redeem and even rescue youngsters but I have never before encountered the imagery of innocent children swept up in a tragic refugee crisis.

As I looked at the art and heard the Joneses stories, I knew that these images could give voice to the scope and breadth of the tragedy in very particular ways. As is often true, when we listen to children or, in this case pay attention to what they draw, the emotional, cognitive and developmental consequences of their experiences are made clear. It is my hope that this investigation of the art helps expand awareness of these children's experiences as they are relocated across our planet for political reasons they do not (and actually none of us) fully understand.

There are a few themes that I would like to identify to organize my observations. As an art therapist, I look at color, composition, vibrancy and symbolic communication.

Overall I was initially struck by the amount and placement of the color blue, often dominating, dividing or interrupting the composition of the pictures. Sometimes the blue clearly and unquestioningly depicts water, sometimes it governs the picture, sometimes it intrudes into the imagery jolting the viewer and sometimes its charged boldness indicates the power that the water must have had on the children's consciousness. As we remember that many of these children came from desert countries and had likely never or rarely seen large bodies of water, their travel across the Aegean must have penetrated their imaginations.

As I continued to look more closely I became aware of a frequent divide or a gap between two separate sections of the drawing. It was interesting to see how often it was the color blue that either integrated or further divided the components of the drawing. Sometimes the image was bifurcated by a representation of a body of water that had to be navigated,

and sometimes the drawing was divided into inside and outside space by a structure that seemed both protective and vulnerable. In general the imagery often suggested relocation, travel or change between two different places or two different states of being.

I never stopped noticing the vibrancy of the drawings, the way they frequently filled the whole page and used many colors. It appeared that the children were eager to make the imagery, eager to express themselves, full of stories that needed to be told. The art is full of life, of emotion and of a need to self-express. How wonderful that the Joneses greeted the children with paper and markers at this moment in their lives. In the vibrancy we also notice the kind of resiliency that reminds us of the capacity of the human spirit. Despite their wet exhaustion, the children exuberantly engaged with the art process and expressed themselves. Above all else, this moved me deeply.

And finally I was curious about the symbolic or metaphoric communication utilized by many of the children. In particular I noticed the frequent representation of houses; small ramshackle houses, large complex castles, anxiously drawn minimalist structures, houses clustered in neighborhoods, houses isolated and alone, house after house symbolically representing each child's unique and defining experience.

How do these observations of color, composition, vitality and symbolism help us and even more importantly help these children? It is my belief that the more we pay attention to the children's expressions, the more we are compelled to share and engage in solution-seeking conversations.

May the art of these children and the publication of this book help us connect to the experiences of others who seem far away and inaccessible. May we all deepen our encounters so we, too, cannot turn away. May we all follow the compassionate response of Robin and Robert Jones.

Dr. Linesch has been the program director of Loyola Marymount's Graduate Department of Marital and Family Therapy for many years. She is the author of many articles and five books, including *Adolescent Art Therapy, Art Therapy with Families in Crisis, Celebrating Family Milestones through Art Making, Facing Genesis*, and *Midrashic Mirrors: Creating Holiness in Imagery and Intimacy*. She developed Art Therapy in Mexico in collaboration with Universidad Iberoamericana, an intercultural training, research and service endeavor that continues to engage students in a summer experience in San Miguel de Allende. She is currently establishing a research institute within the department and is interested in developing non-traditional art therapy inquiry and clinical processes.

To learn more about Dr. Linesch and her activities, please visit her website:
http://debralinesch.wordpress.com/updates/

Map of Lesbos

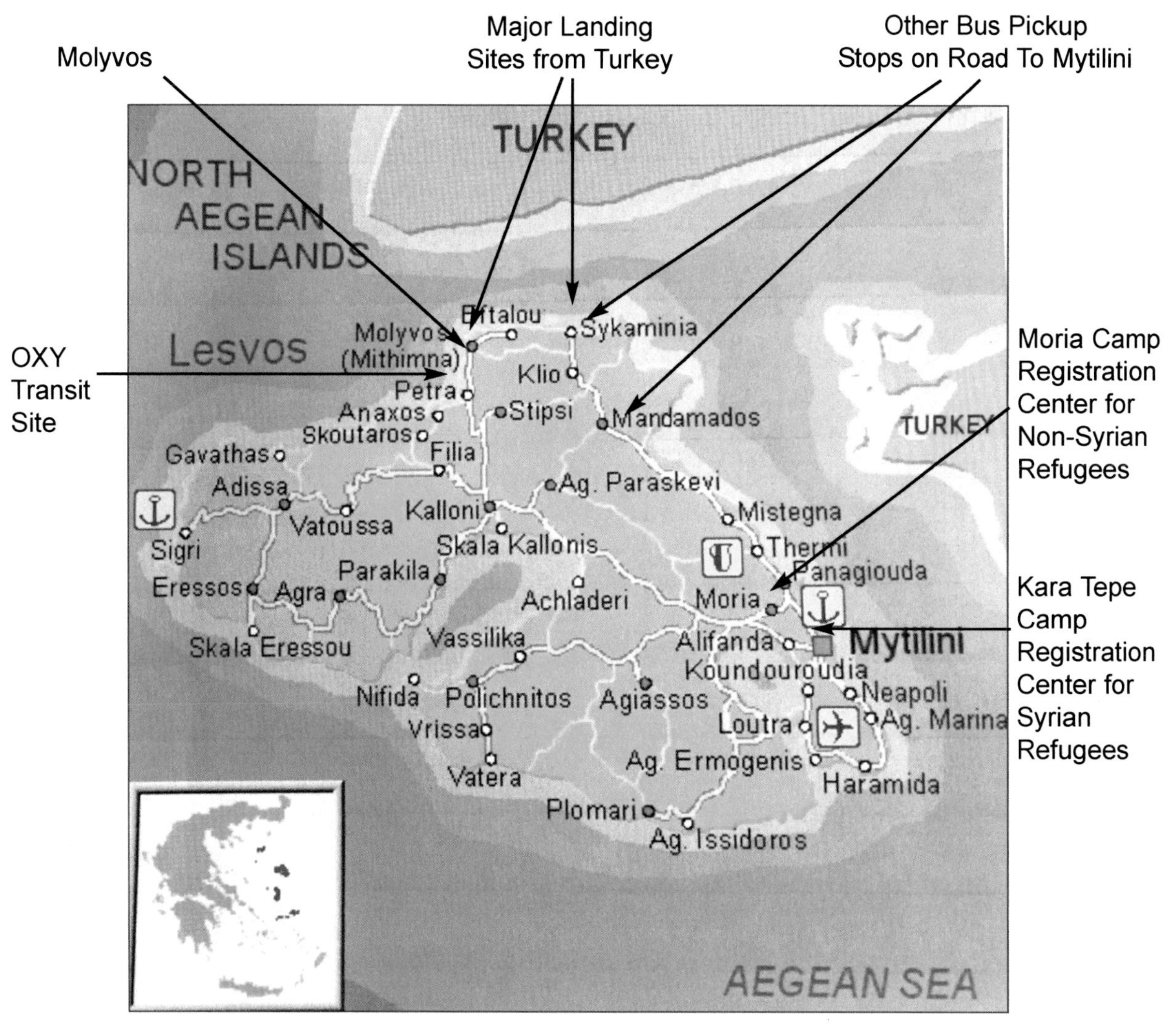

Distances to Formally Register at Camps in Mytilini:

Molyvos to camps:	60 km (37.5 miles)
Sykamania to camps:	40 km (25 miles)
Mandamados to camps:	30 km (18.75 miles)

The Refugee Crisis: Through the Eyes of the Children

Lesbos, Greece April - November 2015

Molyvos, Lesbos

Each return to Molyvos has been different. But this time there is a new *difference.*

The abandoned Byzantine citadel still rests magnificently on top of the village. The villagers and the tourists are here, yet the vast differences between them hasn't changed much. In the forty plus years we have been part of the island, the smell of oregano still permeates the air. The sea moves from a clear blue to steel-grey between unexpected whiffs of wind, and that hasn't changed.

This *new difference* was a world event unfolding on the beaches surrounding the small village of Molyvos

Powerful words and pictures were sent out for the world to see rubber rafts arriving with hundreds upon thousands of human beings seeking refuge on a strange shore. This was an exodus that threatened to overwhelm our village and our island, an unprecedented migration that has shaken the foundation of the entire European Union. Robin, with Nikon and iPhone in hand, tried to capture the difference. I have tried to do the same with words. We do not want to forget.

Molyvos is the quintessential Greek village. It sits on the edge of a small fingertip of land surrounded by thousands of olive trees; the blue Aegean Sea filling in the entire coastline. On a clear day you can spot the white spire tops of minarets along the Turkish mainland with your naked eye. In the morning haze the island floats so close to Turkey that it is difficult to imagine the danger of the narrow strait that divides the two countries and their distinct cultures.

A raft filled with refugees approaches the shores of Molyvos from the Turkish coast, clearly seen in the background, a distance of only 5-7 kilometers (3-4 miles).

Outside the harbor the sea looks calm but rarely stays that way. Without warning the wind rises and white foam laces the tops of rough, short waves. Only the fishermen seem to know when the sea will become treacherous and even they are occasionally surprised at the rapidity of the change. Beyond the harbor, outside the calm of the jetty, the abrupt cliffs of the northern shoreline predominate. The water along the base of the cliffs is shallow and undersea boulders are dangerous predators to unknowing sailors.

It Began As a Trickle In April and Early May

At first there were ten, twenty then forty refugees arriving a day. The first small groups were predominately single men, the occasional woman with a toddler was an oddity. They were all obviously out of place and humbled by their predicament. They were refugees, not tourists; their clothes were neat but well worn. iPhones and even iPads were common. Lack of luggage was the norm; wet clothes and being without shoes were not a rarity. You immediately sensed the anxiety of some, joy in others and weariness in all. Who they were or exactly what country they were from wasn't much of an issue. What to do with them and how to cope with what they needed was a much higher priority.

There simply were no government officials or organizations prepared or available to help as the refugees continued to come and the trickle became 100-200 per week...then 100-200 per day.

The immediate concern was dry clothes, water and a bit of food. Where they might stay or rest was secondary. Small groups gathered at the harbor where there was a single outdoor toilet, an occasional phone charger and a small harbor patrol office where refugees were required to register their arrival in the European Union. The port officials who worked there tried to help. But within a month they were overwhelmed and the registration process had to be moved to Mytilini, 60 kilometers away.

A group of early refugees waiting on the road. Molyvos is in the background.

They Looked Like Orange Streaks On The Water

The rafts appeared orange when we first spotted them among the waves because all we could see was the sun reflecting off the bright lifejackets. There was a raft filled with refugees wearing dark blue lifejackets but no one noticed.

We called them *rafts*. The term may help define our feelings about the armada inundating our shores. They might better be described as pontoon boats. They were definitely inflatable rubber rafts rather than boats yet they floated most of the time. A small motor, a three-piece fiberglass centerboard for some stability, a braided rope hand-hold on some of the more sophisticated models allowed an overcrowded passenger count of 20, then 45, 70 or even 80 when heartless smugglers pushed on additional families. At most the rafts were designed to hold six to eight seated passengers, but of course there were never any *seats* to begin with. The heavy rubber-like material sat deep in the water, just 12 inches from the sea to the upper edge of the bathtub-shaped rim. It required constant, ineffectual baling from even the smallest of waves that soaked the passengers clinging to each other during the dangerous crossing from Turkey to Greece. The pontoons were so low in the water that only the tops of the waves and the mountain range of the distant island filled the horizon.

Can anyone swim? Are there vast oceans in Afghanistan, Iran, Iraq or central Syria that have trained the children, the wives, mothers and sisters covered in the traditional dark colored chadra who are entering the sea for the first time? The fear of drowning in a cold place far from home is somewhat eased by the bright orange "life vests" they can purchase before boarding. The bright orange promises hope; hope that this part of their journey, while still terrifying, is presumed safer than the homes they have been forced to leave behind. Orange shouts out SAFETY with its bright color, its clash with the grey of the cold sea and the false comfort that *I will not be lost*. Most of the vests were counterfeit and tragically useless.

As you can see in the photograph on the left, many of the vests were only filled with a thin layer of styrofoam.

The warnings attached to the children's vests have labels in English-French-German-Spanish, but not in Arabic.

Throughout the months the flow increased. Sometimes the volunteers wouldn't have time to move one boatload of refugees up from the beach before a new boat landed. As storms began in October, the smugglers started packing the refugees in old, rotting wooden boats that were often more dangerous than the rafts. Many split apart and too many people were lost in the sea. One day I saw seven overloaded rafts on the horizon through my binoculars. Two people had fallen in the water and there was no way to help them or alert others to help. Fortunately they survived that day, rescued by another raft.

The whirl of the helicopter blades reverberating off the stone walls of the village took on a new meaning. This sound, a sound you feel, was no longer the simple distraction of tourists disturbing our quiet nor was it the hope that politicians or rock stars were flying overhead with their cameraman bringing attention to this plight. This was now the sound of searching for survivors, the sound of sorrow.

One of The Many Steep Climbs

The walk from the remote beaches where the rafts landed is mile after mile of continuous incline before reaching a paved road where hopefully transportation (which was rare) to the reception centers across the island could be found. Most had to continue walking to Molyvos and later, even further to the transit/rest stop at OXY.

The small town of Klio, just south of where the dirt road intersects the paved road, sits at the top of one of these arduous climbs about 15 kilometers from Molyvos. There is little to attract tourists to this old village. But there is a modern cheese factory and its parking lot serves as the public bus stop. Unfortunately the buses were forbidden to allow refugees to board because by definition refugees were illegal.

Klio wanted nothing to do with a refugee transit stop and put up signs telling them they could not stop there; these same villagers offered bottles of water as the refugees passed by.

The next and larger village was Mandamados, ten kilometers further south, where some of the early refugees staged a "sit-in" demanding transportation to Mytilini so they could be registered.

Eventually a rest/transit stop was created outside of Mandamados by *Doctors Without Borders* offering relief and occasional buses to the registration centers 36 kms away. But at first, everybody walked.

Volunteers, predominantly young foreign tourists visiting the island and hoping to help during this obscene crisis, worked tirelessly around the clock. They reached out the first hand to the refugees as the rafts clamored to shore. They distributed the nefarious plastic water bottles, small amounts of food, occasional ultra thin solar blankets provided by United Nations High Commissioner for Refugees (UNHCR). The volunteers provided a frontline sanity to the maelstrom as well as basic guidance on the direction to the nearest form of transportation, which many times meant simply "walk that way." Behind the volunteers were the local heroes: villagers and resident expats doing their best to coordinate the multiple tasks needed to get through the day-by-day needs of the thousands of arrivals.

When the families made it on to the shore, the initial reaction was pure joy.

Why Couldn't I Drive Any Slower?

There were strict laws against transporting refugees in private cars; initially we were limited to handing out bottles of water, fruit and directions to the hoards of people trudging along the roads as we passed. We were not allowed to give refugees rides but most of us who had cars began to ignore this law. Thankfully, due to excessive heat and inhuman conditions, this law was never really enforced.

Robin and I, along with others, would sometimes drive families from the beach to the transit stop at OXY. One time we took a beautiful family of six Syrians who had just gotten off a raft. Mom and Dad were in the back with the eldest son and daughter, the youngest children were stuffed on Robin's lap in the front passenger seat with one straddling the gear shift I was trying to work. It was a chore loading them all into our small Fiat. Although thankful for the ride, I could see in the rearview mirror how tired and unsure they were. Strapping Robin and the two children into the front seat, trying to get the seatbelt to lock and cease its annoying warning bleep is never effortless but necessary on the dirt path that winds along the rough coastline.

We tried to talk as we drove but limited English and our clueless understanding of Arabic got in the way. Simple words were repeated, "Thank you, thank you!" They looked out the car window and the clear view of Turkey across what appears as a flat sea, reassured them that they were safe; they had survived.

The children were usually cold

We asked if they were okay (with thumbs up), and they replied in understandable gestures. We were able to experience their crossing: the cold, the waves, the constant water coming over the bow and the fear.

The children were cold so we cranked up the heater even though we were in the midst of a warmer than usual October. They smiled—no, they beamed—in appreciation.

"We are here; we made it. We are safe. We can rest," the father communicated to the children. At his voice and his gestures I slowed the car further. They were so thankful for the ride; they had no idea how short it would be.

We continued down the road passing more and more exhausted refugees walking toward the transit stop. The bus was supposed to be around the next curve but in actuality it was still another 45 minutes to an hour's walk for most. The father and mother began to realize there was something unnerving in the sheer numbers of people we were passing. They tried to ask us what is next. I kept apologizing that we were taking them such a short distance.

Robin turned on the radio for a little music to charm the children, passed out sesame sweets and made silly hand signs and facial gestures. Turning towards the parents she tried to explain that we were taking them to a transit station where another bus would take them across the island. The only clear message was that *somewhere* across the island they could be registered, registered for what, we couldn't clearly communicate. What would happen next, we didn't really want to communicate.

I tried to drive even slower, stretching out our time together, allowing them a longer moment of rest. We could have made the drive in 15 minutes as we had done so often in the past few weeks. But we knew where we were really taking them, and I wondered why the car couldn't go any slower.

We helped as the rafts arrived, or we picked up small groups as they walked along the steep road toward the bus stop.

We knew how little we were doing; packing the car filled with often wet, always grateful refugee families, giving them a moment of warmth and hospitality.

Then, for many, the exhaustion and reality set in. They had hoped there was someplace for them to go but it took a while to make that happen.

MIGRANT or REFUGEE?

The words migrant and refugee are constantly commingled. What is the politically correct word for this tsunami of people arriving, these uncountable stragglers along the road? When do you use which term and how many words can you use to define thousands of desperate people you see arriving every day? The children are always described as *the children* but all the rest are bunched into categories: *migrants, refugees, those people* or *them*. You see *them* everywhere. You watch *those people* drop empty water bottles and discard candy wrappers on the side of the road.

Migrants are looking for a job, while *refugees* are fleeing for safety.

Memories of Turkey's 400 year rule had not been forgotten

We distinguish between them by our preconceived ideas. The *migrants* with large families dressed in worn out clothes, carrying garbage bags filled with any personal possessions they had been able to keep are obviously from Afghanistan or Pakistan. The seemingly educated *refugees*, walking proud with newer western clothing, sunglasses and iPhones must be Syrian or Iraqi.

No one really knew. But they all needed help.

The villagers and expats gathered used clothing; locals and tourists showed up with boxes of crackers and fruit purchased at the local markets. Melinda and Theo, owners of the Captain's Table restaurant in the harbor found a way to donate bread and cheese.

There was no place in their small restaurant to have any of them sit down and rest. This would have been inappropriate since they were there illegally, refugees, not patrons. Many in the village feared that these strangers were Muslims, not good Christians like themselves. Unpleasant memories of Turkey's four hundred year rule over Greece had not been forgotten.

Melinda saw people needing help and kindness. What started as a little bread and cheese turned into a small table next to her restaurant that began giving away stacks of sandwiches—ingredients donated and constructed by volunteers—plastic cups filled with fruit juice and bananas. Within days the table turned into a tent and then a place was found where hundreds of refugees could rest overnight, dry their sea-soaked clothes and briefly catch their breath.

Unfortunately, simply by virtue of their presence, the refugees began to draw the attention of visiting tourists away from shopping, relaxed dining and the income the villagers desperately needed. Tourists began to help. Many shopkeepers were not happy.

Maybe It WAS Their Cell Phones?

Many of the refugees asked to use electrical outlets to charge their phones. It was the means to let family you left behind know that you were safe. But the phones also became beacons to the millions left behind that Greece, and Molyvos in particular, was a safe and welcoming place, a landing site from which you would not be turned away. Certainly that's what many of the villagers believed.

The number of refugees making the crossing continued to increase. We had no idea what was coming.

Were the cell phones the cause of our current situation, the beginning of thousands of refugees descending on our small village? "Absolutely!" as most of our Greek neighbors argued. "If you treat them well and let them charge their phones, all they will do is call back to Turkey and tell everyone Molyvos is the place to come. Let them broadcast that and, **mark my words, thousands will come. Thousands!**"

As of December of 2015, 436,000 refugees had landed on the island of Lesbos, according to the *Wall Street Journal*.

OXY Was Born

Melinda McRostie founded the Starfish Foundation in October 2015 to raise money for supplies and take donations to help the refugees

Melinda came up with an idea and successfully negotiated with the owner of OXY to move the constant flow of refugees outside the village. They had been forced to sleep on the sidewalks leading into the village, in the schoolyard and many times in the street itself as the arrival numbers mounted.

OXY, a shuttered disco just a few minutes south of Molyvos, had an empty parking lot. It was turned into a temporary shelter and a transit stop for whatever number of buses that might show up. By the third day there were already two portable toilets, a makeshift tent for the food and three huge tarps stretched from the hillside to the center of the parking lot for a semblance of shade and minimal protection from the coming rain. Beneath the tarps the ground was covered with bits of plastic sheeting and worn blankets crowded with men, women and children trying to find a space to sit or lay on the ground. The refugees, exhausted from the crossing and in most instances many hours of walking, searched for a pickup point for the non-scheduled buses that occasionally arrived.

The OXY Transit Stop

The transit stop was not a bus stop because there was no bus schedule. It was a temporary gathering place for a longer journey, a stop you couldn't justify calling a rest spot as they had no idea how long they would be there. The refugees filled the dirt parking lot and spread into the street. Soaked clothes were placed on sheep fences and guardrails to dry in the sun, but if a bus arrived there was little time to collect anything or you risked losing your spot on the bus. Losing your spot on the unscheduled bus could mean a wait that might cost you a chance to make it to Germany or another northern EU country before yet another border closed.

The Children Began to Draw

OXY quickly expanded with the flow of refugees. Robin was there from the beginning with lots of colored pens and big pads of paper for the children. Only hours after their harrowing experiences crossing the choppy and restless Aegean Sea, the children were suddenly presented with something they could recognize and, for a few brief moments, feel normal.

Robin usually looked for a spot outside the tents; it was too hot to sit inside, the air almost too heavy to breathe. If she found a tarp on the ground or pieces of discarded cardboard, she carefully unfolded her checkered blue Greek tablecloth and laid out a pile of colored felt pens. She motioned to a passing child or a young brother and sister sitting a few feet away as she pulled out a sketch book and imitated drawing on the bright white sheets of paper.

In the beginning the children were a little shy but intrigued with the idea, they couldn't resist a moment to be a child. The children began to draw.

While the children drew they seemed comforted by the normalcy of the moment. They forgot the world around them, the uncertainty and the confusion. Their parents stood or sat quietly in the background. They watched their children draw, smile and laugh and, for the moment, regained a small amount of strength. Their children were safe—for now.

The children created the most amazing art. They drew imposing mountains, cloudless skies, the thunder of passing tanks, apple trees and rubber boats filled with orange life vests. Streaks of blue represented the sea they had just crossed; hope is in every foreground. It is all in their drawings. We could feel their innocent desire to share where they were, where they had been and where they wished to be.

Dealing With The Buses

Loading the unscheduled buses that arrived became a priority for the small team of volunteers. A lost spot on a bus meant a two-day walk to the registration camp across the island, a trek for a young man, a heartbreaking challenge for a child.

With limited resources, the volunteers came up with the idea of colored tickets for the buses and it worked. Each arriving refugee was handed a small square of colored paper: blue, yellow, green, red or black. When we ran out of colors, small paper squares with numbers or simple drawings of trees, flowers, etc. were used. A corresponding square of the color or design is put on the windshield of each arriving bus to make it easy to know which bus to board.

Volunteers help load the buses and give out free tickets

The buses were first paid for by private donations, then thankfully the UNHCR and the IRC (International Rescue Committee) became involved. Almost overnight we had buses arriving on a decent schedule. The two- to three-day walk across the island was being replaced by relatively comfortable coaches leased from local tour companies; the refugees had a ride and the local economy was being kick-started by a new source of income. The refugees' needs were being substituted for the disappearing busloads of tourists that were avoiding the island. Assistance was becoming a business.

The buses were filled as they arrived. There was no need to wait for passengers as they were already lined up, sometimes on a 24-hour basis. There are only 65 seats and hundreds, and some days thousands, were waiting to board.

We learned it was important to stay calm when you are trying to pack as many refugees as the driver will allow on *his* bus. One driver wore a gauze mask to protect himself from *them*. Another driver offered sips from his water bottle to a child. The coach was the driver's world and he offered it begrudgingly or openheartedly: his decision.

Important things to remember when you are loading a bus:

- Always smile or offer an upbeat shrug when loading the bus, it is the only way to communicate.
- Touching offers comfort to some, an unexpected insult to others.
- When standing firm always say "Sorry" with your hand gently touching your heart.
- Answer constant questions in a language you don't speak but we all understand.
- "No. This bus does not go to Athens. We are on an island."

No matter how you load the bus, at least there were buses!

This little boy would not let go of his life jacket.

Meeting One of the Syrian Refugees

Robin comforted a young Syrian woman sitting with her husband outside the stuffy, packed white tents set up by UNHCR. Inside the air was stagnant, filled with the foul smell of wet clothes, unwashed bodies, soiled diapers and discarded rotting food. Every space was littered with dirty blankets, piles of trash and empty plastic water bottles. Families huddled together in the heat waiting for their turn to line up outside for the fabled and unreliable bus to take them across the island. People rested on pieces of cardboard covering the hard dirt floor trying to get a moment of sleep, exhausted from the journey they were really just beginning. Children played in the dirt, slept in their mother's arms or like their fellow travelers fell asleep in the turmoil, heads resting against the few wet backpacks that survived the crossing.

Sahar Kharsa from Syria with husband

Sahar Kharsa, six months pregnant with her first child, shared how she cried every day in Syria. Her husband was an engineer and his work required moving around the city on a daily basis. Cell reception was scattered and every time he didn't answer she would break down in tears. Was he killed, was he kidnapped or was he picked up off the street and forced into some unknown rebel group and sent to the front line? Everyday he thankfully returned and as he came through the door she would smother him with kisses and thank Allah he was alive.

They knew they couldn't live with the constant fear and could not bring their future child into a life of such horror. They had to leave Syria; they had to make it to a better life.

You can watch Robin's interview with Sahar at www.throughtheeyesofthechildren.com

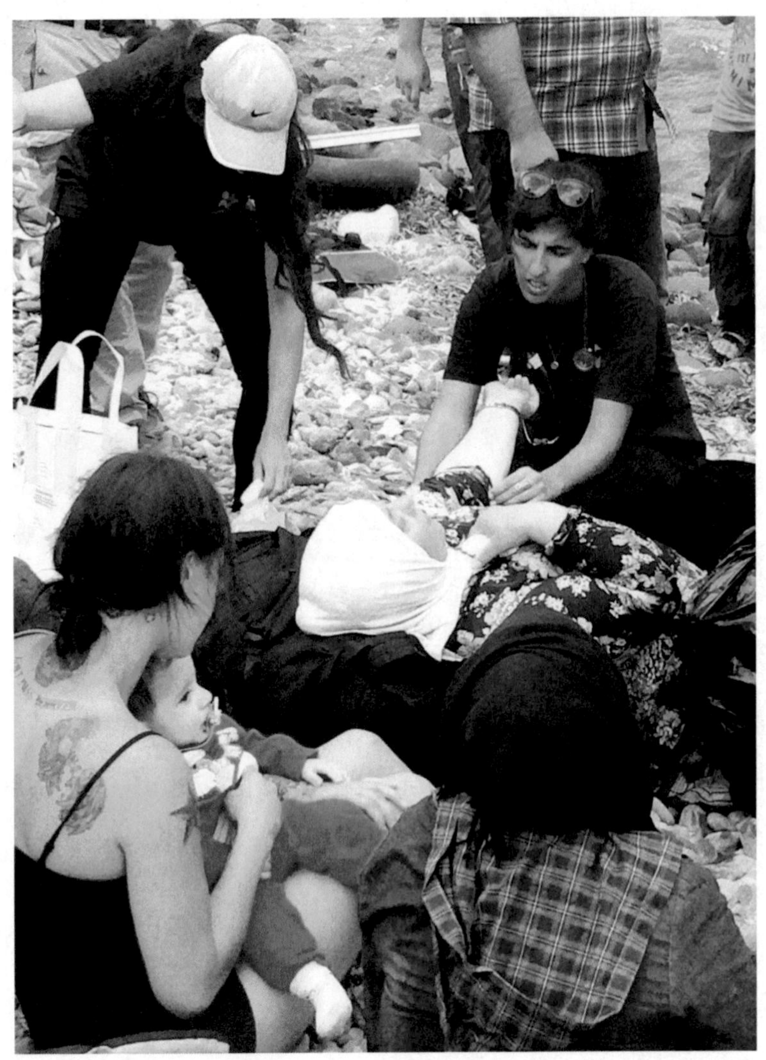

Tali Shaltiel, MD, with IsraAID, worked tirelessly with other NGOs and volunteers to treat injured refugees

International Organizations Arrive

The NGOs (Non-Governmental Organizations) started to arrive over the summer. *Doctors Without Borders/Medecins San Frontieres* (heroes all) set up a small emergency clinic consisting of two folding tables, six chairs, a 10′ x 12′ tarp for shade and three or four portable medical field kits. There were sandwiches and water bottles available while the wait for the bus began. Women, children, the elderly and families were given priority on the bus. The volunteers were constantly guiding the loading of the buses and making every possible effort to ensure that no families were broken up or children left behind. Young men who were traveling without family began yet another walk to the next stop, five or so miles away to allow room on the bus for families. Segregation by country of origin did not begin until late September when the registration camps across the island began to overflow.

IsraAID medical personnel arrived early in the crisis and helped so many, especially the elderly and children injured during the crossing. They were always on the beach administering triage, bandaging cuts, wrapping sprains. Whatever was necessary, they were always there. You could count on their smiling faces to calm any situation.

Tali Shaltiel, 31, (shown below center and on the facing page) a physician from Jerusalem in her dark blue IsraAID shirt, was in the thick of administering to the injured. That brought questions from some. As she was treating an older man, he asked a friend who was comforting him, "Why is a woman helping me? She's from Israel!"

His friend replied, "You are lucky to have such good people to take care of your wounds."

UNHCR provided tents, emergency blankets and the very much needed transportation. Other aid organizations followed. They were all greatly appreciated. But the actual care and feeding of the refugees in Molyvos and OXY continued to be done by small groups of volunteers.

Refugees arriving at OXY

Although the original *invitation* from the northern countries had been intended for Syrians, it was heard and accepted by war-weary people from Afghanastan, Iraq, Somalia, Eritrea and even Pakistan. All who came to Lesbos eventually ended up at the processing centers in Mytilini. Two camps had been set up, one for Syrians and Palestinians named Kara Tepe and another for everyone else called Moria.

By October 1, 2015, after we finally had regular bus service, the order came to load the refugees on the buses based on their country of origin so the refugees would go to the appropriate processing center. There were so many arrivals that it was impossible for the buses to drop people off at both centers. It was up to the volunteers to load the buses properly and to make it clear that if you were not Syrian, not to get on the bus for Kara Tepe because you would be turned away and have to walk the six kilometers to Moria.

The Registration Camps: Kara Tepe and Moria

A refugee registering with officials

A little girl shares a smile

Moria Camp was a former prison

We visited both camps. Kara Tepe's (the Syrian camp) registration and processing center, was uncluttered and clean with crisscross paths divided by chain link fences. There were designated areas for minimal medical care, playgrounds, tented areas for temporary shelter, basic food and water provisioning. Although fenced in, the gates remained open. After registration the government allowed travel in Greece but how you traveled was up to you; there was no system in place to assist. Your only way off the island was to purchase a ticket on the Athens-bound ferry and space was extremely limited. Departure off the island was just the beginning of a long journey to the North.

Entering the "other" camp outside the small village of Moria was a different story. Large triple gauge wire fencing and a steel-enforced entry gate were topped with coils of razor wire. The gates, like the simpler ones in Kara Tepa, were open and unlocked, for now. It is a camp that was previously a prison and we can only hope it does not revert. Moria Camp is where smiles disappear as reality and fatigue overwhelms the memory of joy and relief felt when the raft first touched the shoreline.

Moria is overcrowded, chaotic and sanitation is extremely limited. No one can tell the refugees how long they will be there. Families know better than to get separated. Moria is a day away from *there* and an abrupt halt to the dream of here.

Who Would Bring Their Children Into This Danger?

What does it take to risk everything? The wind does not stop; the horizon is filled with wave after wave after cresting wave.

All we can do is hope no one tries to cross today, yet they do. It is always the orange life vest against the grey sea, and the hope that someone on the boat has an idea of what to do. Can they ride the crest of each breaking wave? Is the raft slowly deflating in the pounding sea?

My heart tries to skip a beat so that I can hold the binoculars steady. I exhale as I focus on the horizon, always the horizon, a wavy line that makes Robin slightly seasick whenever she looks into the glasses.

I pray not to see a streak of orange, yet I am like a hunter hungry for the prey. The prey is helpless but hopeful.

Perhaps the children will remember the kindness of strangers in Molyvos and OXY and will hold on to the hope that there will be a better future.

Through the Eyes of the Children

How The Children's Art Came To Be

The drawings that the children created provide us with a unique perspective of the "refugee crisis." As Dr. Debra Linesch points out in her insightful introduction, the children see hope but the sea crossing has a major impact on many of them.

As Robert explains in the book, Robin took her art materials to the transit stop and, as English was rarely spoken, no direction of what to draw was given. Once the children realized what they were being invited to do, they quickly joined in. Robin mimed drawing and sometimes sang the alphabet song or said the names of colors. Mainly they communicated with lots of smiles, thumbs-up and hugs.

All of the art was created within hours of landing.

The children often had to leave abruptly with their parents without finishing their art when their colored bus ticket was shown. It meant it was their turn to board the long-awaited bus to the registration camp across the island, to yet another unknown destination.

Robin photographed many of the children to record their smiles and to later connect them to their art. The children reacted positively to the camera. They gathered around her to get a chance to proudly display their efforts and get their photo taken holding their drawings.

Robin was surprised when she offered the drawings to the children to take with them; they almost always waved their hands and heads back and forth to say, "No."

Robin was gifted with an extraorindary collection of the children's original art, some of which is included here.

افغانستان

One of the most powerful of the children's drawings shows tanks shooting at people, the boat crossing the expanse of the sea to a world of trees, birds and flowers. The frowning sun above is replaced with a smiling sun in Lesbos. Note the figures in the water that seem to suggest not everyone on his boat survived the crossing.

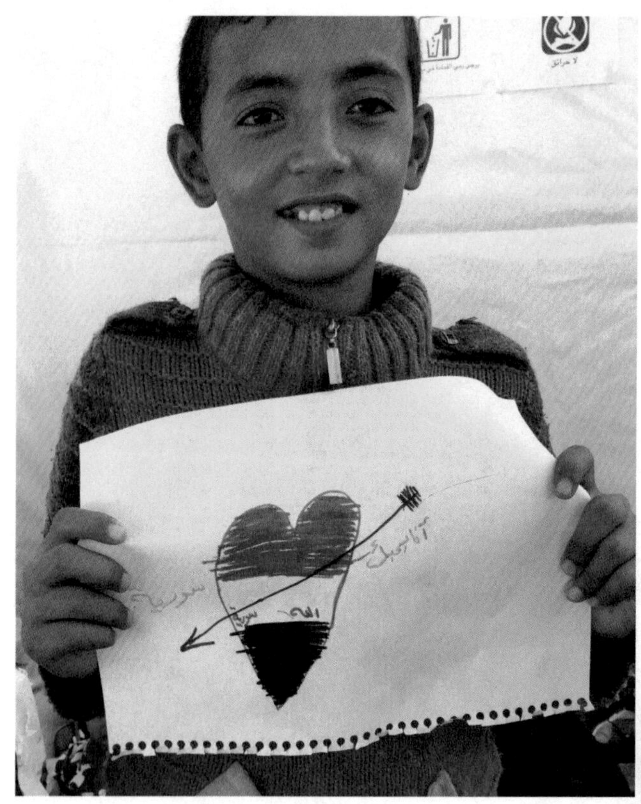

Some drew hearts. The one on the left seems to represent the Syrian flag...with an arrow through it.

Some drew homes.

Flowers and the sun with the vertical blue streak (the sea) leading to a new life are a constant theme.

WISE GUYS
National
سورية
بلدي
الأردن

The Crossing

سورية يا حبيبتي
my Love

سورية حبيبتي

One of the few drawings that several children worked on together.

What lurks beneath the sea.

The approaching boat is full of orange vests and discarded ones can be seen along the shore.

shanti
Asma

moadese
ILOVE
Afghanestu

Naughty Cat

ΔΗΜΟΣ ΠΕΤΡΑΣ

A promised world full of bright colors,
windmillls, ice cream and happiness.

The eyes and smiles speak of hope.

Afterword

What Does An Orange Beach Cost?

A strange question to ask when you are standing on the beach road outside of Molyvos on a typical windswept afternoon. In the spring of 2015 it was a deserted drive on a bumpy dirt road that runs parallel to the sea, nothing between you and the clear azure water but a narrow rocky beach and the occasional pepper tree. You can usually see the tops of minarets on the Turkish side. Today the beach is different; today it is orange. Not from a paint spill or a brilliant sunset, it is orange because the rocky shoreline is covered with abandoned life vests.

Thousands upon thousands of orange life vests liter the landscape; the color broken only by hundreds of black, blue and yellow vests. Plastic water bottles, discarded wet clothing, empty gas cans, soaked shoes and abandoned boat paddles fill any empty space.

Volunteers created enormous piles of now worthless lifejackets so that later the vests—momentarily someone's only hope in case of a dreaded capsize—might be hauled to some imaginary waste site. Within hours hundreds more surround the newly created piles and again cover the beach in color. The orange was replenished day and night by the arriving refugees; even the sea can't sweep the vests away.

Deflated black rafts also litter the beaches of the "orange coast."

These small motors provided power for the overloaded rafts.

The deflated hulls of the black pontoon rafts, semi-covered in sand and stone comically remind you of hundreds of Pacific elephant seals basking cozily in the sun, but there is nothing funny here.

The smugglers charge between $1,000 - $1,500 per person for a crowded minivan trip from Istanbul to *somewhere* along the Turkish coast, just within eyesight of Greece, usually Lesbos. Refugees are packed into the inflatable rafts for the slightly more than five kilometer crossing to the island. The hope is that the smuggler does not get lost or abandon you. You pray that enough gas was put in the small fuel tank to complete the voyage.

Orange life vests are optional, up to $100 each; children's yellow safety vests go for $50, and you can drape an inflated inner tube over your shoulder for $25. Many discarded children's vests are labeled: **Not For Use In Boating. Not A Lifesaving Device**. We hope that the flotation device found on this beach indicates that the child who used it arrived safely. Occasionally the vests arrived alone.

There are black life vests a quarter of an inch thick that are simply a thin slice of Styrofoam covered in cloth. A cheap plastic strap and buckle decorates a blue vest filled with straw or cotton batting that acts more like a sponge than a buoyancy device; the brightly colored safety whistles attached to them look like they come from Cracker Jack® boxes.

So how much does this orange beach cost?

From April to the full moon in September 2015 over 200,000 refugees and migrants have entered Greece, almost all by water. More than 60 percent have landed just outside Molyvos.

By early December the number rose to 436,000 on the island of Lesbos alone. If we assume that 60 percent of those landed outside our village, that is 261,600 refugees.

If the average price of the passage from the Turkish coast was $1,250 and each refugee purchased an orange vest, another $100, the total per person would be $1,350.

$1,350 x 261,600 = $35,316,000

At these prices, why stop the flow?

Dealing With What Was Left Behind

The young volunteers never stop, and I am caught many times wondering what I can do to help while they move from moment to moment doing everything they can to ease the transition for others. They appear organized, not from any orders from above, more from trial and error, repetition and a knowing that they must keep going. Fueled by the needs of others they go on, hour after hour, day after day, helping in the mundane ways that being on the front line really means. They signal a raft to maneuver away from treacherous rocks; they steady a pontoon beating against the shore as sixty unsteady human beings try with some dignity to land on foreign soil; they lift an infant onto the beach, put out a steady hand to let someone know they are safe, hug a shivering child and take the time to offer a bottle of water or dry clothes to all arrivals. There are days I stand shoulder to shoulder with these young warriors hoping for a perfect future.

There Are Days I Just Need To Be Alone. On Those Days I Pick Up Trash.

Picking up bits and pieces of the moment is, if nothing else, a breath of sanity in a place where reality has become a bit too real. On a good day I have Greek-blue garbage bags with sewn-in plastic yellow ties, surgical gloves and my own private strip of beach that is overwhelmed with trash from multiple landings. For the moment it is deserted. I wander for hours, filling bag after bag with exodus-like debris dropped on the beach by the multitudes of humanity seeking a safe haven. Into my bag goes that extra water-logged shoe, a silken head scarf, a comb, a spoiled diaper, packets of multicolored pills that may be seriously needed. Small plastic bags filled with sweetbreads are discarded next to soaked pamphlets of the Prophet's blessings and guidebooks filled with simple translations from Urdu to English. Sunglasses that will not make the journey are dropped

in the excitement of arrival. All are collected along the shore. I touch and feel each item before placing it in the trash bag with the yellow plastic tie.

There are always other items that must be disposed of with little thought. Open, half-eaten cans of unfamiliar sardines warmed by the mid-August sun, more water-logged diapers, salt-soaked undergarments, piles of excrement in any shadowed spot—behind the medical tent or under a blanket soiled by the toll of crossing. Left over bits of inedible sandwiches and multiple banana peels lie in the summer sun, covered with discarded sweaters, coats, t-shirts, name brand bluejeans and flies—millions of flies. Everything is damp, stiffening with the seawater that claimed so much from so many. All collected along with plastic water bottle after plastic water bottle, rotting pieces of fruit and still more hidden piles of excrement. Everything goes into the blue plastic bags.

There are the thousands of life jackets abandoned on the beaches; yellow, blue, black, orange, child floaties and deflating tire inner tubes. Most were useless when they were worn; now there are piles of them everywhere. Is there a responsible way to make it all go away? What do you do with over 200,000 discarded brightly colored, now totally worthless life jackets?

The vests are taken by dump trucks and overloaded pickup trucks to a rocky tire-puncturing dirt road, past a dilapidated donkey farm with no donkeys. In a vacant valley overlooking the scenic beauty of Molyvos the bulldozers are digging an enormous pit in which the life jackets are dumped day after day. The bulldozers never rest.

When Robin and I returned this year the landfill had tripled in size to a mountain of rotting vests and broken boats that had been hauled up the road and dumped beside the pit. Hulls with gaping holes and splintered decks, lifeboats broken in half lay lifeless in the midday sun. The eerie landscape, an ecological graveyard of hope and promise, is now cluttered with the remains of boats that may or may not have carried their passengers to a safe landing.

For the moment, the beaches are clean again.

Acknowledgements

Our Deepest Gratitude to:

The Sponsors: **Laurie** and **Rabbi Arthur Gross Schaefer** and the **Avi Schaefer Fund**
Thank you for following through on your dream to do everything in your powers to help manifest this book and help spread this message to the world.

Debra Linesch, PhD of Loyola Marymount University.
Thank you for embracing the importance of sharing the children's images and understanding their deeper meaning. We truly appreciate your very poignant Introduction for this book.

Dearest **Cathy Feldman**, Blue Point Books, publisher/book designer
Your skillful talents, patience and clear vision inspired us from beginning to end!

Special Thanks to:

Congregation B'nai B'rith Santa Barbara and Community, especially to the *Refugee Aid Committee* and *Sisterhood of Salaam and Shalom.*

The Saint Barbara Greek Orthodox Church and Community

Mavis Manas with the *Hellenic Journal*

The Santa Barbara Independent, especially Tyler Haden for his extraordinary cover story, *Horror and Hope on Lesbos*
www.independent.com/news/2016/mar/10/horror-and-hope-lesbos/

Dr. Richard P. Appelbaum, MacArthur Chair in Sociology and Global & International Studies, University of California at Santa Barbara

Dr. John W.I. Lee, Department of History, University of California at Santa Barbara

Gordon Sichi, Headmaster of Anacapa School for creating the Synthesis Unit 2016, Human Migration: The Search For a Better Life

It really *Takes a Village*

We give thanks to ALL the extraordinary people of Molyvos who rode the wave and later tsunami of refugees arriving on our shores, month after month, with compassion and strength, showing up day and night on the beaches and harbor with clothes, food and open arms.

Thank you to the many fisherman who were out saving lives in place of making a living catching fish, shopkeepers who personally drove truckloads of bread and nourishment to temporary stations, set up along the coastline, when the call came that people were desperately in need.

Thank you **Andriotis Thanasis,** Molyvos-President Elect, who works tirelessly on the daily needs of our village and oversaw the many tasks that kept our village running smoothly in the face of such a storm.

Thank you **Timothy Jay Smith** for organizing the donations of many urgently needed items including 10,000 hats to cover the heads of refugees walking across the island in the blazing sun, at a time when there were no buses.

Thank you **Melinda McRostie** for stretching your neck out further than anyone knew was possible. The people who watched you in action 24/7 will always remember your heart. You are a fabulous human being and always a friend.

Our Beautiful Island

The charter flights from Europe have all but stopped arriving on Lesbos. "The Island of the Refugees," as many now refer to Lesbos, has almost completely lost its main source of income, tourism. Please come to Lesbos and experience her unique beauty and meet the very special people who are waiting to welcome you.

From Crisis Management to Sustainable Living

IsraAID, founded in 2001, is a non-profit, non-governmental humanitarian organization committed to providing life-saving disaster relief and long-term support. For over a decade, our teams of professional medics, search & rescue squads, post-trauma experts and community mobilizers have been first on the front lines of nearly every major humanitarian response in the 21st century. One of IsraAID's trademarks is its ability to draw from ever expanding networks of highly experienced professionals representing the diverse Israeli population.

When a natural disaster strikes, time is of the essence. Every passing hour dramatically reduces survival rates and hampers recovery efforts. IsraAID responds immediately, with their relief teams among the first to arrive on the ground, providing life-saving medical care, food and supplies, as well as cleaning and construction materials.

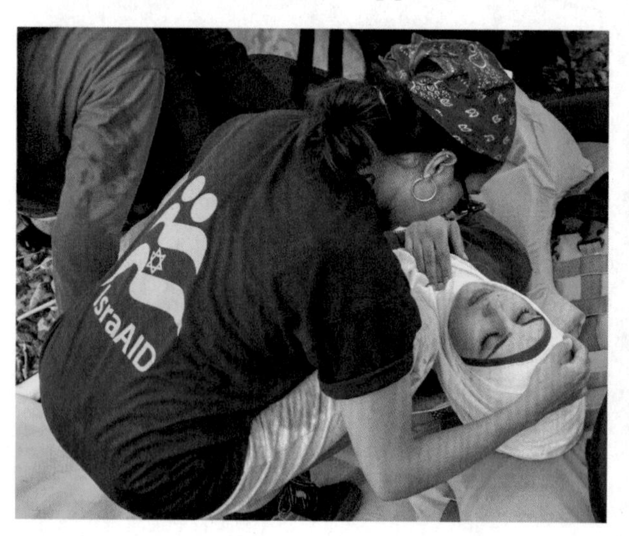

In over a decade, we have...

- Responded to crises in 35 countries
- Reached over 1,000,000 people
- Distributed over 1,000 tons of relief and medical supplies
- Trained more than 5,000 local professionals
- Mobilized over 850 staff, volunteers, and professionals (a majority of them doctors, nurses, therapists and social workers).

Focus on the Syrian Refugee Crisis

In 2015, increasingly large numbers of asylum seekers started to flow through Greece on their way to Western Europe seeking refuge. Authorities in Greece were rapidly overwhelmed as over 850,000 arrived on the beaches. Routes became more and more treacherous and risky, with the Aegean Sea in particular becoming a graveyard for countless families, especially children. IsraAID is responding to this crisis as it evolves.

IsraAID's team in Lesbos is a multi-faith group including Muslims, Christians, Jews, Druze and Yazidi, from Israel, Palestine, Germany, U.S., U.K. and Iraq. The team has been working together since August 2015, and so far more than 120 Jews and Arab volunteers joined the life saving efforts.

Photographs courtesy of IsraAID

Avi Schaefer

The Avi Schaefer Fund (ASF) is dedicated to nurturing Avi's values of mutual respect and understanding through cultivating opportunities for informed dialogue and by empowering young people to be change-makers in the world.

Before his tragic death, Avi was involved in a variety of projects to promote understanding and peace between Israelis and Palestinians. His passion for this work stemmed from a deep, abiding love for the Jewish people coupled with a commitment to the safety and security of the State of Israel and of all people in the region. Avi believed deeply in the possibility of forging a lasting peace between Israelis and Palestinians. His open heart and generous spirit shaped him into a compassionate and empathetic human being. The Fund will be guided by Avi's memory as it develops and supports projects that work toward the fulfillment of his dream of peace. We are always looking for ways to promote understanding and carry on Avi's vision.

When a terrible earthquake hit Haiti in December 2009, Avi was home on winter break from Brown University. Sending money to various relief agencies was a natural reaction. But Avi mobilized his community of friends to produce a fundraising event back on campus that would fulfill several goals: highlight the work of Israeli NGO IsraAID, which was already on the ground in Haiti with a team of doctors and other professionals; raise funds for IsraAID; and bring together people who wanted to help. As Avi imagined this fundraising effort, he dreamed it would start at Brown and then catch on at other campuses across the country, highlighting the important work of IsraAID and raising awareness about the need in Haiti. The event put on by the students at Brown University took place on January 12, exactly one month before Avi was killed by a drunk driver.

The funds raised that night went to IsraAID. Unfortunately, Avi's dream that other campuses would create similar events to raise awareness and relief funds ended when Avi died.

When I saw a presentation by a representative of IsraAID and heard Robin and Robert Jones tell their story about the refugees in Lesbos, I was so moved I wanted to support their efforts in any way I could. Robin's penetrating and colorful photographs depicting the refugees in their desperate journey toward freedom touched me deeply. These children had seen so much in their short lives and their experience was a nightmare. I immediately thought about Avi, his effort to raise awareness about IsraAID and the important work they do around the world and his dream that the fundraising effort he began at Brown would be an example to other students across North America. The idea to sponsor a book of the children's drawings, along with Robin and Robert's experiences on Lesbos with the Syrian refugees, seemed a natural way to further Avi's dream. I hope this book will encourage others to do similar projects on their college campuses and in their communities.

Laurie Gross Schaefer
Co-founder, Avi Schaefer Fund
Santa Barbara, California

About the Authors

Robert has been traveling the world since he was 18 years old. He has owned an Asian art gallery and bookstore in Toronto, Canada, is a SCUBA instructor, a poet, and was President of an international processing and distribution company.

Robert and Robin Jones in Molyvos

Robin holds a BFA and Teaching Certification from Temple University (Tyler School of Art in Philadelphia) and is passionate about family, photography, cooking, and travel (among many other things).

In 1974, on a break from their separate worlds, they met by chance on the Greek island of Hydra. From there they traveled by ferry to the island of Lesbos and the beautiful village of Molyvos.

Robert and Robin married in Toronto and returned to Molyvos later with their ten-day-old son for 14 months.

After ten years in the corporate world, in 1987 they retreated back to Molyvos, now with their three sons for a year's sabbatical.

Returning to the States, the family moved to Santa Barbara (where Robert had gone to high school) and started a successful travel company that recently sold after 28 years. During those years they frequently returned to Molyvos, and in 2007 bought a second home. They continue to spend 3-4 months a year there.

Robert and Robin are blessed with three wonderful sons; Michael, David and Joshua; four grandchildren; Eloise, Emmeline, Orion and Atticus, and last, but definitely not least, three amazing daughters-in-law: Dana, Beppe and Samantha.

They treasure the years they spent building and running their travel company together, especially since the business gave them a further excuse to continue traveling with their children and enable them to learn firsthand the value of other cultures and the importance of engaging with the wider world around them.

Robin and Robert's lives were forever changed by the refugee crisis. They knew while this crisis was unfolding that beyond the words and photos, it was an extraordinary moment for them personally to get a chance to experience the profound gift of caring for other humans in desperate need. The shared smiles, hands touching hearts in thanks and the wet eyes will never be forgotten.

Made in the USA
San Bernardino, CA
10 October 2016